# AMERICAN REVOLUTION

Troll Associates

# AMERICAN REVOLUTION

by Francene Sabin

Illustrated by Robert Baxter

**Troll Associates**

*Library of Congress Cataloging in Publication Data*

Sabin, Francene.
    American Revolution.

    Summary: Explains the causes of the American
Revolution and traces events leading to the surrender
of the British general Cornwallis at Yorktown in
October 1781.
    1. United States—History—Revolution, 1775-1783—
Juvenile literature. [1. United States—History—Revolu-
tion, 1775-1783] I. Baxter, Robert, 1930-      ill.
II. Title.
E208.S25      1984          973.3        84-2582
ISBN 0-8167-0136-9 (lib. bdg.)
ISBN 0-8167-0137-7 (pbk.)

It is early morning, April 19, 1775. Armed American colonists known as the "Minutemen" have gathered on the village green at Lexington, Massachusetts. They are waiting for the British troops, who must pass Lexington on their way to the nearby village of Concord. The British are planning to destroy the colonial supplies of arms and ammunition at Concord. But the Minutemen have other ideas.

Now the British troops are in sight. Tension builds higher and higher. Suddenly, the early morning silence is shattered by the sound of gunfire. With the first shot— the "shot heard round the world"—the American Revolution has begun.

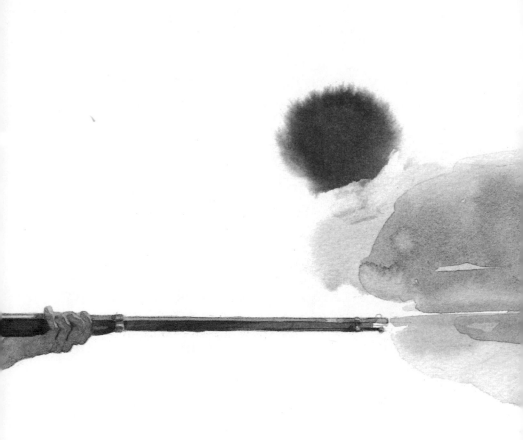

The war was bound to come. For many years, the colonists had been growing angrier at the way Great Britain treated them. When the Colonies were first established, there had been very little interference from the British government. As the Colonies began to prosper, however, Great Britain's demands increased.

Heavy taxes were imposed on colonial imports and exports. The British Parliament passed laws restricting colonial trade with other countries and forbidding the colonists from manufacturing certain products. The more the colonists proved able to take care of themselves, the more Great Britain tried to keep them dependent.

Heavy taxes and trade restrictions were not the only causes for the American Revolution. The colonists had carved a new world out of the wilderness and had become a new people in the process. They were more self-sufficient than their cousins in the Old World, and this gave them a sense of independence. When Great Britain began to make excessive demands, the American colonists realized just how self-sufficient they had really become.

Another cause for the war was the presence of a forbidden frontier to the west. Just when the Colonies had become secure, well settled, and ready to expand, Great

Britain closed the frontier. This action, in the form of the Proclamation of 1763, ruled out any settlement or trade west of the Appalachian Mountains.

The British said they did this to prevent further wars with the Indians. But the colonists were sure that it was an attempt to keep them under tight control and dependent on Great Britain. At the same time, there was no drop in the number of immigrants moving to the New World. The population was growing, but the Colonies were not.

Among the colonists' greatest complaints were a series of laws passed by Great Britain. These were the Sugar Act, the Quartering Act, the Stamp Act, the Townshend Acts, and the Intolerable Acts.

The Sugar Act placed a tax on molasses coming from the French and Spanish West Indies. That meant the colonists had to buy molasses from the British Indies or pay the penalty of a high tax. The colonial protest against taxation without representation began with the Sugar Act.

The Quartering Act required that the colonists provide food, housing, and supplies to British soldiers stationed in the Colonies.

The Stamp Act placed taxes on newspapers, legal documents, and many kinds of business contracts. Colonists had to buy tax stamps to put on these items to make them legal.

People in the Colonies protested so strongly that the British Parliament repealed the Stamp Act. But they said that they had the right to tax the colonists in any way they chose. Parliament then passed the Townshend Acts, which taxed colonial imports of paper, paint, lead, glass, and tea.

Taxes on tea led directly to a colonial action known as the Boston Tea Party. This took place in December 1773, when a group of Boston citizens, some of whom were disguised as Indians, dumped boxes of tea off British ships into Boston Harbor.

The British were furious. Parliament then passed the Intolerable Acts. As a result, Boston Harbor was closed, and the city was placed under blockade and martial law.

People in the other colonies rallied in support of Boston, sending food, money, and encouragement to the besieged city. Still, the colonists tried, at the first Continental Congress, to reach a reasonable compromise with Great Britain.

The Continental Congress pledged loyalty to the Crown and asked that the abuses against the Colonies be stopped. The British answer was rejection, backed by more harsh laws. This left the Colonies with little choice but to fight. And the sparks at Lexington and Concord ignited the powder keg of the American Revolution.

The Continental Army, as the American army was called, consisted mainly of untrained, poorly disciplined, and inadequately armed bands of local militia. While most of them knew how to handle a gun, they knew little else about soldiering.

The British military forces were well trained, well supplied, and well organized. They also heavily outnumbered the Continental troops. In addition to the Redcoats, who were regular British army troops, the British forces included Loyalists, mercenaries, and various Indian tribes.

Loyalists were colonists who sided with the British. The mercenaries were soldiers from other countries who were paid to fight for Great Britain. Many of the mercenaries were called Hessians because they were recruited from Hesse, in Germany. The Indians fought for England because they knew that a colonial victory would mean an American expansion into their territories west of the Appalachians.

Great Britain's advantage was even greater at sea. The British had a large fleet of warships and a well-trained navy. The colonists started the war with no navy at all and no fleet. So until a fleet could be built, the Americans used privateers in the war.

A privateer is a privately owned ship that carries arms. A government may authorize such a ship to make war on an enemy's fleet. A privateer is free to keep the ships and goods it captures at sea.

The idea of using a privateer navy was suggested by Captain John Paul Jones. This

saved the Americans the cost of building a large fleet. And until the new United States could put together a real navy, the privateers fought the war at sea. The Americans never had as many ships as the British, but they finally succeeded in defeating the Royal Navy.

The land war—fought with rifles, muskets, and cannons—was waged in New England, in the southern colonies, and in Canada. The earliest battles—at Lexington, Concord, and Bunker Hill—took place in New England. By the time the Declaration of Independence was signed on July 4, 1776, the war had expanded up into Canada and down into North and South Carolina.

In Canada, the colonists hoped the French-Canadians would join forces with them against the British. Although this didn't happen, the Americans did manage to keep large numbers of British troops busy fighting in Canada and northern New York.

The commander of the Continental Army, General George Washington, concentrated almost one-third of his troops in the Middle Atlantic states, between Massachusetts and Virginia. Some of the fiercest engagements were fought around New York City, throughout New Jersey, and into Pennsylvania.

During the winter of 1776, the Continental Army was at its weakest. They had lost a series of battles. They had little food, clothing, and military supplies. And they were suffering from exhaustion. They needed something to rally their spirits.

General Washington supplied that "something" on Christmas Eve 1776. He led his troops from Pennsylvania across the icy Delaware River to stage a surprise attack on Trenton, New Jersey.

There were about 1,400 Hessians encamped in Trenton. By the next day, more than 900 were prisoners of the American army. The daring raid gave heart to the colonial troops. It helped to sustain them through the long, bitter winter at Valley Forge.

In spite of losing battles at Brandywine, Germantown, and elsewhere, the Americans were gaining strength. From the beginning, France had been secretly aiding the colonists against Great Britain. Then, in 1778, France entered the war and sent a fleet and an army to fight on the American side.

Yet even before this, the Americans had been aided by many foreign volunteers. These included the Marquis de Lafayette from France, Baron de Kalb from Germany, Count Casimir Pulaski and Thaddeus Kosciusko, both from Poland, and Baron von Steuben from Prussia.

Slowly the tide of the war turned in the Americans' favor. With the aid of the French fleet, British supply lines were cut. Now the English, not the Americans, were growing short of military supplies.

The final battle of the Revolutionary War was staged at Yorktown, Virginia, between British troops under General Charles Cornwallis and a combined French-American force under Washington.

For two weeks the combat raged. Finally, on October 19, 1781, the British surrendered, and Cornwallis turned over his sword to the victorious Americans.

Except for a few minor skirmishes in the south and along the western frontier, the war was over. But it was not until September 1783, that the United States and Great Britain signed the peace treaty, in Paris. After eight-and-a-half long years, the American Revolution had ended.